GREAT SALT LAKE

Past and Present

by

DAVID E. MILLER

Copyright by D.

Salt Lake C

GW00703198

Fifth Editic
Revisio
Anne Miller Eckman
and
Lawrence L. Eckman

Additional copies postpaid anywhere in the United States.

Anne M. Eckman
315 North 800 East
Bountiful, Utah 84010
801-292-4632

Lithographed in the United States of America
PUBLISHERS PRESS
Salt Lake City, Utah

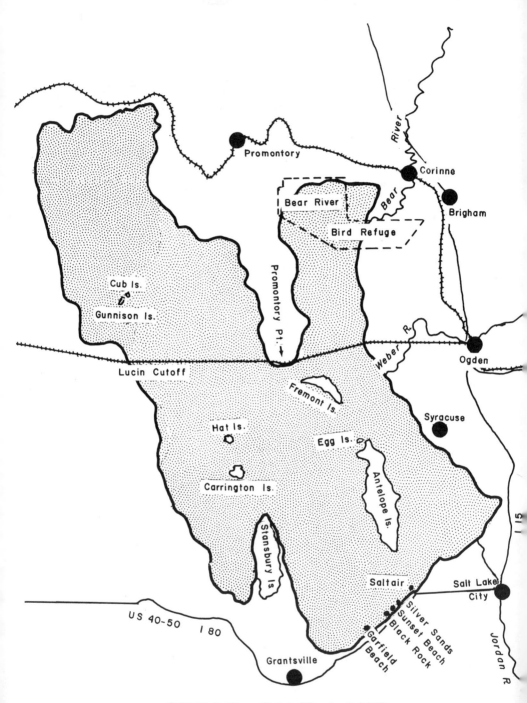

GREAT SALT LAKE

2

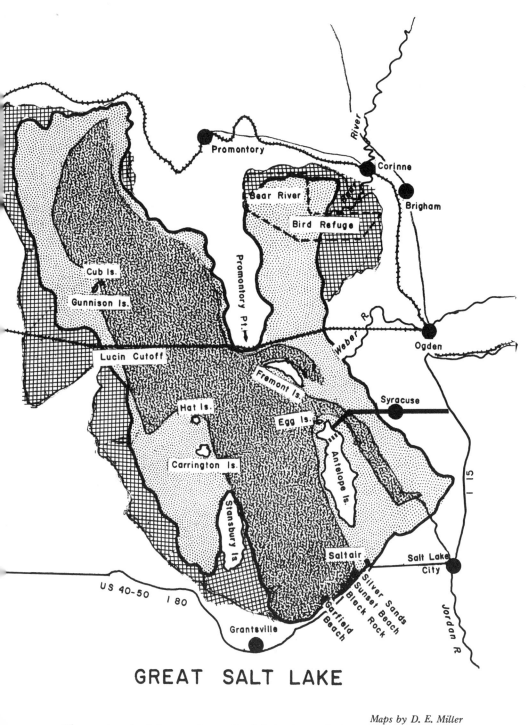

GREAT SALT LAKE

Maps by D. E. Miller

The center shaded area shows the lake's size and shape at its lowest level (1963). The outer shaded area (squares) shows the shape and size of the lake at its highest level (1873). Also shown are the major resorts at the south end of the lake and the Syracuse road leading to the north end of Antelope Island where the Great Salt Lake State Park was opened in 1969.

TABLE OF CONTENTS

INTRODUCTION

There has always been a great deal of curiosity and an air of mystery about Great Salt Lake. Long before it was discovered by Jim Bridger rumors of it had acquired fantastic proportions. And long after the lake had been completely explored some of these weird tales were still perpetuated. A powerful lake tribe was said to inhabit the lake islands; large whirlpools, marking the opening of subterranean channels that drained the lake into the Pacific Ocean, and kept it at a constant level, were believed to be located in its midst. As late as 1870 "eye witnesses" reported such a whirlpool between Antelope and Fremont Islands and stated that "a schooner was almost drawn into it." Fears were expressed for the safety of steamers then cruising the lake. Today there are only a few inches of water where this incident was said to have occurred.

Every lake must have its monster, and Great Salt Lake is no exception. Rumors of the monster helped shroud the lake in mystery. In 1877 a group of workmen camped at the north end of it reported that the monster came bellowing out of the lake and invaded their camp, causing them to flee to the hills. Next morning huge overturned boulders showed clearly the trail left by the beast.

Most fantastic of all was a Provo, Utah, newspaper account (1890) of a school of whales swimming and spouting in the lake. This is such a naive story that it merits recounting in full.

Intelligent newspaper readers have not forgotten the inauguration fifteen years ago by Mr. James Wickham . . . of the whale industry in the Great Salt Lake. As considerable time was required for the development of the experiment the subject has passed out of the public mind but it has by no means been forgotten by naturalists or capitalists interested in the whale fishery. The whale is the largest and probably the longest lived animal. They have been known to grow to 100 feet in length and live to the age of 400 years. It is a mammal, or, in other words suckles its young. The project of Mr. Wickham was greatly assisted by this fact, for the difficulty that would attend the obtaining of whale eggs in the deep seas is at once apparent. It was only necessary to obtain a pair of whales in order to begin the propagation of the animals under domestication. The southern or Australian

5

whale was selected as the best suited to the Great Salt Lake. The greater part of two years were occupied off the coasts of Australia by a vessel sent especially for the purpose in continued efforts to capture the young whales without injury. The feat, however, was at last accomplished, and the beasts, each about thirty-five feet long were shipped to San Francisco in 1875 in tanks built expressly for them. Fifty tanks of sea water accompanied their overland shipment to insure plentiful supplies of the natural element.

Mr. Wickham came from London in person to superintend the "planting" of his leviathan pets. He selected a small bay near the mouth of Bear River connected with the main water by a shallow strait half a mile wide. Across this strait he built a wire fence, and inside the pen so formed he turned the whales loose. After a few minutes inactivity they disported themselves in a lively manner, spouting water as in mid ocean, but as if taking in by instinct or intention the cramped character of their new home, they suddenly made a bee line for deep water and shot through the wire fence as if it had been made of threads. In twenty minutes they were out of sight. . . .

Though the enterprising owner was of course, disappointed and doubtful of the results, he left an agent behind him to look after his floating property.

Six months later Mr. Wickham's representative came upon the whales fifty miles from the bay where they had broken away, and from that time to the present they have been observed at intervals, by him and the watermen who ply the lake, spouting and playing.

Within the last few days, however, Mr. Wickham cabled directions to make careful inspection and report the developments, and the agent followed the whales for five successive days and nights. Discovering that the original pair are now sixty feet in length, and followed about by a school of several hundred young, varying length from three to fifteen feet. The scheme is a surprising and complete success, and Mr. Wickham has earned the thanks of mankind.

Catching whales in Great Salt Lake and following that business on the dangerous Greenland coast are two quite different things. The enormous value of the new industry can be better appreciated by remembering that a single whale produces twenty tons of pure oil.

There have been many other myths and legends connected with the lake. Of course, scientific study and exploration disproved most of these rumors and replaced false information with facts—facts just as fascinating as the myths. But there is still a great deal of misunderstanding about the lake and its history and a general lack of accurate easily accessible information about it. Interest in the lake is as great today as it ever was; everybody wants to learn the truth about it. In this booklet you will find the information you have been seeking.

DESCRIPTION AND GENERAL INFORMATION

	4,200' Level	4,211.85' Level
Length	75 miles	85 miles
Area	1,500 sq. miles	2,400 sq. miles
Greatest depth	30 to 40 feet	40 to 50 feet
Mean depth	13 to 15 feet	15 to 20 feet
Salinity	25%	5 to 18%

America's Dead Sea, the Great Salt Lake, is one of the major geographical and geological features of the world. It has been an important factor in the development of the West. Jim Bridger, Peter Skene Ogden and many other famous Rocky Mountain trappers examined its shores in search of beaver streams; Kit Carson and John C. Fremont explored it; to California gold-rushers it was a serious barrier that had to be by-passed. Since the coming of Brigham Young and the Mormons to its shores, the lake has assumed economic value; hundreds of thousands of tons of salt have been extracted from its brine; scores of boats have been launched on its waters; its islands have been occupied and put to use, primarily as grazing lands.

Great Salt Lake is the largest body of water in the United States west of the Mississippi and occupies the bottom of the largest closed basin in North America (the Great Basin). It is the largest salty lake in America. The lake is a sheet of water some 75 miles long and 50 miles wide, the surface of which is approximately 4,200 feet above sea level. This elevation places the surface higher than the average elevation of the Allegheny Mountains. The length and the width, hence the area, vary greatly with the seasons and with the cycles of lake oscillation.

Since the lake is almost completely surrounded by flat plains barely higher than its water surface, a slight rise in the water level extends its area considerably. It is estimated that a ten foot rise in the lake would cover an additional 240 square miles of plain. Since

Howard Stansbury's Great Salt Lake Survey (1849-50) the water level has varied as much as 20 feet (see graph pp. 24-25), altering the shoreline in some places as much as 15 miles. The highest level of the lake, since 1850 when the first records were made, was in 1987 and the lowest in 1963, the area varying from a high of 2,400 square miles to 1,420 square miles. In 1987 the area was 69% greater than in 1963.

The lake is fed by numerous rivers and small creeks, the principal streams being Bear, Weber, and Jordan Rivers. Strange as it may seem, the lake was almost as high a century after the arrival of the Mormons as it was in 1847, this in spite of the fact that some 800,000 acres of land are being irrigated with water diverted from the various streams that feed the lake.

The depth of the lake has not varied as radically as has the area. This is because a slight increase in depth spreads the water over an extensive plain. Howard Stansbury sounded the lake completely in 1850 and found no place deeper than 36 feet. In 1873 water 48 feet deep could be found; in 1963 the deepest water was about 26 feet. Since the lake is so shallow, having a mean depth of only 13 to 15 feet, any appreciable drop in level exposes sand bars and makes peninsulas out of islands. Hence, some of the "islands" have changed their status several times during the past century. The earliest Mormon exploring expedition on the lake—the *Mud Hen* expedition of 1848—impressed with the shallowness of the water, branded the lake "The Briny Shallow."

Rise and fall of the lake also affects the relative salinity of its water; when the water is high the salt content decreases. This rule applies to spring flood seasons as well as to cycles of several years of high or low water. In 1850 Stansbury found the saline content to be 22.4%; in 1873 (the extreme high water mark) it was only 13.7%; in 1963 it was approximately 26%. This means that there is one pound of salt for every four pounds of water; the weight of a gallon of lake water is one-fifth greater than that of fresh water. At extremely low levels the water reaches the saturation point and salt is precipitated in the quiescent shore waters. Early explorers and settlers in the Salt Lake Valley often used the lake water as brine for preserving meat. It is estimated that the lake contains some 8,000,000,000 tons of salt.

The salt content of Great Salt Lake water is about the same as that of the Dead Sea in Palestine (which contains 23% to 25% solids) and is nearly eight times as salty as ocean water. This dense lake water has an appreciable effect on floating bodies. Boats built for use in fresh water ride high on the briny surface. The brine is so dense that it buoys at least one-fourth of the human body above the surface of the water. Since Brigham Young and a few

8

"Iceberg" in Great Salt Lake. This one was 30 feet high.

Mormon explorers first swam in it late in July, 1847, the lake has become famous for swimming. Few visitors to the Salt Lake region care to miss the opportunity of swimming in the lake where one cannot sink.

In spite of the concentrated saline quality of the water ice is often formed on parts of the lake. Of course, the lake brine does not freeze; it is far too salty for that. What actually happens is that during relatively calm weather, fresh water from the various streams flowing into the lake "floats" on top of the salt water, the two failing to mix. Near mouths of rivers and creeks this "floating" condition exists at all times during calm weather. During the winter this fresh water often freezes before it mixes with the brine. Hence, an ice sheet several inches thick has been known to extend from Weber River to Fremont Island, making it possible for coyotes to cross to the island and molest sheep pastured there. At times this ice breaks loose and floats about the lake in the form of "icebergs." It has been known to do damage to boats and other vehicles used in and about the lake. One of the largest icebergs on record formed in 1942 when the ice broken up by wind piled up to a height of 30 feet and a width of over 100 feet and floated about the lake. Interested people visited it and climbed about on it with complete safety.

Although the lake is usually described as "beautiful" when viewed from a distance, it loses much of its glamor upon closer examination. Lack of trees, bushes, and grass along most of its shoreline gives the lake the true aspects of a *dead sea.* And these shores become wider and wider as the lake decreases in size until at close range about all one can see of the lake is a broad strip of salt plain and mud with a thin ribbon of water way off in the distance. This condition exists along most of the shoreline except at the south end where excellent bathing beaches of fine sand are located. This long flat approach to the lake is often edged by a strip of black mucky mud that emits a most offensive odor. Fremont noticed it in 1843 and Stansbury gave an excellent account of it in 1850. He found it to "consist almost entirely of the larvae of insects lying upon the bottom . . . and seemed to be impregnated with all the villainous smells which nature's laboratory was capable of producing."

This brings up a point often misunderstood by most people, that of life in the lake. Of course, no fish can live in the concentrated brine, but other life does thrive in it. The larvae referred to above develop into a species of small fly or gnat so common around the lake. In the water itself, a tiny brine shrimp is found. This is a pinkish orange-colored creature with relatively large black eyes and five pairs of flimsy, bristle-like legs. It seldom reaches more than a quarter of an inch in length and is usually much smaller. These little animals can often be seen in the calm shallow bays of the lake, swimming about just beneath the surface. At times they are so numerous that they give the water a slightly orange tint. The brine shrimp feeds on a type of green algae that also grows in the lake. The larvae and shrimp are the only types of animal life visible to the naked eye, although scientists have located several species of microscopic life. A sort of sea weed flourishes in the deeper waters.

Naturally, fish drift into the lake, but they die as they reach the lake brine. As salinity decreased with water levels above 4,211 feet, a small species of fish called the Rainwater Killi has been observed in the south arm of the lake.

Although no other fish or wildlife live in the lake, attempts have been made to propagate oysters, fish, and eels at the mouths of streams. Beadle, writing in 1879, pointed out that:

Oysters have been planted at the mouths of the rivers, but when the wind has been upstream, the dense brine setting in from the lake killed them. Jordan was stocked with eels a few years ago, but they floated down into the lake and died. One was picked up long afterward on the eastern shore, completely pickled. The finder cooked and ate it, and found it very palatable.

Probably the earliest reference to the possibility of planting oysters, salt water fish, crabs and lobsters in the lake appears in the *Deseret News* February 5, 1853. This article suggests that the salty bays could be tempered to suit the needs of the various forms of life to be introduced. At the mouths of rivers and in certain bays, artificial dams could be constructed and the salt content of the water controlled by strict regulation of the amount of fresh water running into the embayment. The article contains rather definite plans for the construction of such dams, spillways, etc. It further points out that all types of shell fish as well as salt water fish could live in the same ponds, producing enough sea food to supply all the needs of Utah. Fish would find streams satisfactory for spawning. Shad, salmon, and other salt water fish are mentioned as especially adaptable to lake culture.

Following are a few references of actual *attempts* to plant sea life in the lake. On August 12, 1882 the *Deseret News* carried this item:

> Fish Commissioner Eugene G. Blackford received an order from Henry House at Corinne, Utah for two barrels of seedling oysters which he intends to plant and cultivate in Great Salt Lake when a suitable place can be found.

Much hope was held for the success of the experiment. Two days later the same paper carried a second article:

> An effort is to be made once more to raise oysters in the Great Salt Lake. . . . A thorough trial was made several years ago at the mouth of the Weber River. The seedling oysters arrived in good condition and were planted and tended carefully. But the conditions were found to be unfavorable. Too much salt impregnated the water at a distance from the river, the mud that washed into the lake from the river's mouth was unsuitable to bivalve, and the oysters soon "petered" out leaving not a sign of their existence.
>
> It is possible that Mr. House may be more successful at the mouth of the Bear River, than the promoters of the scheme were at the influx of the Weber, but his attempt is not the first of the kind. We should be very much pleased to be able to chronicle the successful cultivation of the oysters in the great saline lake of the North American Continent.

Another brief reference to these experiments was made in 1891: "Efforts have been made to propagate fish, oysters, etc., in the lake, but without success. They all die."

As might be expected on such an inland sea, storms are common and develop rather suddenly. In such instances the mirror-like surface of the lake is often turned into a raging sea of rolling waves and whitecaps. If possible, lake boatmen avoid sailing during severe storms because the heavy waters create a tremendous strain on boat timbers; several lake craft have been wrecked in such storms. Dense lake waters driven before the wind often rise several inches in a few hours submerging sand bars as well as miles of normally bare plain. Storms come up suddenly and often die down just as suddenly. Waves of the dense water often move heavy boulders on the Lucin Cutoff, making it necessary to keep crews busy constantly reinforcing the right-of-way. Visitors to the lake have often observed an obvious rise or fall of the water and have inquired concerning the times of high and low tide. But there are no tides on the lake. What appears to be a rising tide is merely the result of the heavy water being pushed before the wind.

The Great Salt Lake affords opportunity for innumerable activities and studies. Hunting, boating, swimming and racing help make it a veritable paradise for sportsmen; students find it a fertile field from many points of view—geology, history, anthropology, biology; economists are busy converting its resources into profitable enterprises. It is even useful to the U.S. Government which has used its islands as bomb ranges. Truly, the lake has afforded and now affords varied interests and activities for untold numbers of people.

SWIMMING, BOATING, RACING

Saltair showing bathing facilities when the lake was high.
Courtesy KUED

Saltair In Its Heyday. This picture was taken near the turn of the century when full trainloads of pleasure seekers arrived regularly at Saltair.

Swimming

A swim in Great Salt Lake is a rare experience no visitor to the Salt Lake region wants to miss. Tourists go hundreds of miles out of their way just to take advantage of this opportunity available nowhere else in the world. Everyone can swim in the lake—no one is too old or too young—for no swimming ability is necessary. All you need do is sit down, or lie down, relax and *float*. You can't sink! If you wade or swim out to deep water you can walk in it; the only trouble you'll have is keeping your feet down, for the bouyancy of the water tends to make you float like a log on its surface.

Since the first visit to the lake by Brigham Young and a few Mormon explorers late in July, 1847, the lake has been attractive to water lovers. The exploring party on that occasion went swimming at Black Rock and enjoyed this experience immensely. Numerous bathing resorts have flourished at times about the lake. However, most of them eventually failed, primarily because the recession of the waters left them high and dry.

Although swimmers are warned against diving because the highly concentrated brine is very painful to the membranes of the nose and throat, swimming in the lake is perfectly safe. There is no record of anyone having drowned in it while swimming. The few people known to have lost their lives in the lake have done so as a result of boat wrecks or airplane crashes. Because of the extreme buoyancy of the lake water the best type of livesaving equipment

Courtesy James S. Silver

Reconstruction of the Saltair Pavilion. The lower story became flooded shortly after its opening in 1983. The flooded parking lot served as a boat harbor.

A renovated pavilion was reopened in July, 1993.

Saltair Bathers. This was a common experience at Saltair during the 1920's.

is a ten-pound weight tied to the feet in order that a person might keep his feet down and head up.

Lake Resorts

Numerous bathing resorts have been established around the lake during the past century: Black Rock, Sunset Beach, Saltair, Garfield Beach, Lake Shore, Silver Sands Beach. Most of them have enjoyed years of depression and prosperity, primarily because of receding or rising lake water.

Thousands of Utahns as well as tourists flock to the beaches every summer to enjoy the never to be forgotten experience of swimming in water where a person can float like a cork without moving a muscle.

Largest and most famous of the Great Salt Lake bathing resorts was Saltair, which afforded visitors various sorts of entertainment other than bathing—its dance pavilion and roller coaster were famous in the intermountain west. Originally constructed in 1893 at a cost of a quarter of a million dollars, the resort facilities were remodeled from time to time. Saltair was built on 2,500 piles driven into the lake bed about three quarters of a mile from shore. Access to it was gained by means of a railroad and highway also constructed on piles.

The popularity of Saltair varied with the rise and fall of the lake. When the resort was built in 1893 the lake was reasonably high and white caps dashed against the pilings. The resort enjoyed sufficiently high water until 1930, when the lake dropped to its lowest recorded level, and Saltair was left high and dry. The water fell back several hundred yards from the pavilion. With the rise of the lake during the 1940's Saltair again regained its status as a bathing resort, but with the decline of the lake during the 1960's the once proud resort fell into disuse. It was closed to the public during the summer of 1968, and was destroyed by fire in 1970.

In 1981, construction was begun on a full-sized replica of the Salt Air Pavilion. The nearly completed building was opened in February of 1983, but had to be closed in December of the same year due to the rapidly rising waters of the lake. Extensive diking failed to keep the lower story from flooding. Receding waters permitted re-opening in July, 1993.

Antelope Island and Great Salt Lake State Parks

Antelope Island State Park was re-opened to the public in 1993. It had been closed by the floods of 1983. A 6.5 mile causeway links the island with the city of Syracuse. (Take exit 335 from I-15.) The park affords swimming beaches, camping, boating, and other attractions.

The island was named for pronghorn antelope which were re-introduced in 1993 after an absence of 60 years. Visitors may also observe buffalo, deer, and elk in a natural setting. The annual buffalo roundup begins the last weekend of October and draws visitors from around the world. Also included in the park is tiny Egg Island where thousands of seagulls nest each year.

The State of Utah is also developing Great Salt Lake State Park, encompassing 4.5 miles of the south shoreline extending from Black Rock to the site of Old Saltair. Construction of beach facilities and a new boat harbor has been completed.

Boating

Boating on the lake has been for the purpose of exploration, shipping and pleasure. Explorers such as James Bridger, James Clyman and John C. Fremont had launched various types of boats on the lake before the coming of the Mormons to this region. But exploration did not cease with the Mormon migration. In the spring of 1848 Albert Carrington and the *Mud Hen* crew conducted the first Mormon exploration of the lake and its islands.

This group spent several days exploring Antelope Island, Fremont Island, Promontory Point, and Bear River Bay. Three Indians and a herd of Indian ponies were sighted on Antelope Island. The explorers reported that island to be well supplied with grass and other vegetation as well as numerous springs of fresh water. It was doubtless because of their favorable report that the island was occupied shortly thereafter for grazing purposes.

Boats for the transportation of cattle, sheep, and horses to and from the islands and various parts of the mainland have been used since the 1850's Dozens of craft, both sail and steam, have been employed for that purpose as well as for shipping such products as cedar posts, salt, and ore. Brigham Young's boat, the *Timely Gull,* launched in the Jordan River in 1854, was one of the earliest of these boats. It was designed primarily for the purpose of ferrying livestock to and from Antelope Island. The *Timely Gull* was wrecked in a storm in 1860.

In 1871 the *City of Corinne,* the largest steamer ever to ply Great Salt Lake waters, was launched at Corinne (near the mouth of Bear River) for the purpose of hauling ore from the south end of the lake to the smelter then located at Corinne. This was a Mississippi River type stern-wheeler with a capacity of 240 tons. When the original enterprise failed, the *City of Corinne* was converted into a pleasure craft. As such she sailed the lake for many years making regular stops at the various resorts. People on shore often heard her bands and watched her bright lights as she passed near shore on numerous lake excursions. James A. Garfield visited Utah and sailed the lake on the *City of Corinne.* It is claimed that he was first mentioned as a possible candidate for the United States Presidency while on that cruise. At any rate, the boat was subsequently re-named in honor of its distinguished passenger and cruised the lake for years under the name *General Garfield.*

Literally hundreds of other craft have been used on Great Salt Lake. In 1939 the Salt Lake County Boat Harbor was constructed at the south end of the lake to accommodate the various types of boats that plied the Great Salt Lake waters.

Racetrack on the Bonneville Salt Flats. Speed kings follow the black
line as they whiz over the salt at 600 m.p.h.

Speed on Salt

The world's fastest race track is located on the Bonneville Salt
Flats west of Great Salt Lake and just east of Wendover on U.S.
Highway 40-50; I-80. Almost all the automobile world records for
speed and endurance have been made there. This is one of the few
places in the world where speeds faster than 600 miles per hour
have been attained.

The Salt Flats make an ideal race track. Salt was deposited there
by receding Lake Bonneville waters thousands of years ago and
varies in thickness from a mere skim to several feet. Races are
conducted on the thickest part. The plain is as hard as concrete
and smooth as a floor making an ideal surface for speed. There is
plenty of space and nothing to run into if the car gets out of
control. Nine months of the year the flats are covered by a thin
layer of water from rain and melting snow. The track is not
normally dry enough for racing until August or September. Even
after it is "dry" there is enough moisture in the salt to keep tires
"cool," lessening the danger of blowouts at high speed.

SALT AND SALT PRODUCTION

Where did the salt of Great Salt Lake come from? Geologists
give us the answer. Most rocks contain minute quantities of salt

Salt Lake Yacht Club Harbor. Opened in 1939 and operated effectively for several decades.

that is easily soluble in water. Rain and snow in the mountains, coming in contact with this salt, dissolve it and carry it in solution to streams that eventually flow into the lake. Since the Great Salt Lake is located in an enclosed basin without an outlet all the salt carried into it during the past thousands of years has remained there. Lakes with outlets carry salt out as fast as it is brought in, thus keeping the water "fresh." Because the water from this lake escapes by evaporation only, the salinity of the water tends to become greater and greater since the minerals are not removed by the evaporation process. Hence, it can be asserted that the 8,000,000,000 tons of salt found in the lake was at one time disseminated throughout the rocks of the area that drains into the lake. The rivers are still depositing salt in the lake.

Extraction of salt from Great Salt Lake is one of Utah's oldest industries. The industrious Mormon pioneers established salt boiling vats at the lake within a few days after their arrival in Salt Lake Valley (1847). It was soon discovered, however, that in numerous places, deposits of salt several inches thick had been laid down by evaporating lake waters; this could be had for the taking. Within a few years the idea of constructing artificial evaporation ponds was conceived. It was a relatively simple task to construct such ponds and numerous suitable locations for them were soon discovered. All that was necessary for such construction was to throw up low banks of clay on the flat plains slightly above the lake level. These could be easily pumped full of lake brine; the sun did the rest by evaporating the water. A careful study of the salt deposited showed that sodium chloride (common salt) is precipitated at a certain degree of density and that by controlling the density of brine in the ponds, practically all other (undesirable) salts could be drained off, leaving a deposit of virtually pure salt. This is substantially the system used to extract salt from the lake today.

At harvest time this salt is plowed up and stored in huge piles where it "weathers" while awaiting final processing. Processing takes place in the refinery where, through a process of heating, drying, screening, crushing and packaging, various grades of salt are produced. Salt has more than 1,000 uses; table salt accounts for only a small percentage of the total production. In spite of the vast quantities of salt found here, Utah produces only about 1% of the nation's salt supply.

Courtesy Utah Historical Society
Early Salt Harvest Equipment. This photo shows early salt harvest operations of the Utah-Salduro Company.

Salt Harvest. Plowing a field of salt is one step in the salt harvest. Some 8 billion tons of salt are contained in Great Salt Lake's brine.

Potash From the Bonneville Salt Flats

Potash production is one of the newest industries associated with the Great Salt Lake region and one that holds a great deal of promise for the future. The immense expanse of the Bonneville Salt Flats lying immediately east of Wendover contains almost unlimited quantities of this product which is there to be had merely for the taking. But the extraction of it is quite an undertaking.

During World War I the Solvey Process Company of Syracuse, New York, built a plant on the Bonneville Flats where, from a 30,000 acre tract, brine was collected from which potash was obtained. Operations were successful as long as high war prices prevailed. But the plant closed shortly after the end of World War I. However, interest in potash production didn't die with the closing of the first plant; there were those who continued experimentation on ways to profitably extract potash from the brine. In the late 1930's a new company, Bonneville Ltd., was organized for that purpose. This company controls some 60,000 acres of the flats, which are covered by a coat of salt varying from a thin film to three feet, and has developed an extensive system of canals and ponds for evaporation purposes. In 1992, the Great Salt Lake Minerals Corp. was the largest producer of potash in North America.

Since the 1960's new and energetic plans have been made and operations begun for the extraction of Magnezium Chloride, Sodium Sulphate, Potassium Chloride and Lithium Chloride from the lake brine. Utah's Dead Sea has become a living treasure.

GREAT SALT LAKE ISLANDS

Numerous islands are located in Great Salt Lake. These are, in the order of their area: Antelope, Stansbury, Fremont, Carrington, Gunnison, Hat, Dolphin, Cub, Egg, and White Rock (see map p. 2). At extremely low water levels only Fremont, Gunnison, Egg and White Rock are completely surrounded by water; the others have been surrounded at times and are always referred to as "islands" although they are often in reality merely extensions of the mainland—peninsulas. All the islands follow the general pattern of mountains in the vicinity, being relatively narrow, running in a north-south direction, the large ones thrusting their rocky slopes several hundred feet above the water surface. Four of the islands (Antelope, Fremont, Carrington and Gunnison) have been the homes of settlers at times during the past century. Antelope, Fremont, Carrington and Stansbury Islands have been used as stock ranges and are still very valuable grazing lands. Agricultural crops have been cultivated on Antelope and Gunnison although with completely negative results on the latter. Guano deposits of considerable extent are found on some islands, but attempts to profitably market this product have not been very successful.

Antelope Island—Named by John C. Fremont in 1845

Antelope Island is some 16 miles long and almost 6 miles wide. It lies just a few miles from the east shore near the south end of the lake, and is easily seen from highways north and west of Salt Lake City. Several springs of fresh water are found on its slopes, making it an ideal stock range. A sand bar connects it with the mainland. Soon after their arrival in the Salt Lake Valley, Mormon leaders recognized the potential value of both Antelope and Stansbury Islands and acquired them as grazing ranges. Thousands of horses, cattle, and sheep have been pastured there.

In 1891 George Frary filed a homestead claim on 160 acres of Antelope Island and moved there with his wife and their four children. Frary became well known as a "lake" man who had spent many years of his life navigating and exploring it. In 1897

Ranch House, Antelope Island. This is the oldest building in Utah still being used for the purpose for which it was built.

tragedy struck the family: Mrs. Frary suddenly became ill and died before a doctor could reach the island. Her lone grave, the only one on the island, is still decorated by ranch hands.

One of the interesting features of Antelope Island since the turn of the century is its herd of American Bison. The island had once been the native habitat of both buffalo and antelope but the former had left the island before the arrival of the Mormons in Salt Lake Valley; antelope soon disappeared also. During the 1890's the idea was conceived of restocking the island with

The Charles Stoddard homestead cabin on Carrington Island, 1932. Failure in attempts to develop fresh water led Stoddard to abandon the project.

23

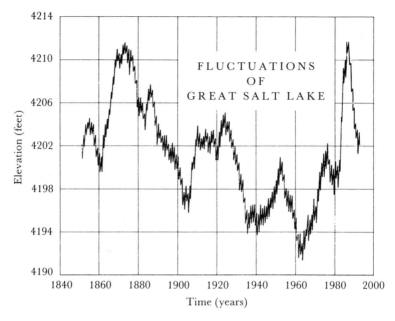

FLUCTUATIONS
OF
GREAT SALT LAKE

buffalo. As a result a dozen head of these animals, purchased in Texas, were transported to the island to become the nucleus of a great herd. One objective was to cross the buffalo with cattle but this didn't prove very successful. Another objective was to preserve the rapidly disappearing "denizen of the plains." This last was more successful, for the small herd soon increased in numbers until there were approximately 300 head roaming the island, much as they had done on the open plains a half-century earlier. In filming "The Covered Wagon" in 1922, Hollywood producers gained permission from the island owners to shoot the buffalo scenes there.

By 1926 the interests of the island owners had shifted definitely from buffalo to domesticated stock and the bison was found to be a handicap. It was then decided to conduct a last great buffalo hunt. Sportsmen from far and near attended, paying $300 each for the privilege of shooting their own game on the island. The hunt was a great success, and the herd was reduced to thirty cows and about 25 calves. Today the herd, managed by the Utah State Parks Service, numbers about 650.

Fremont Island—Named by Howard Stansbury for John C. Fremont in 1850.

Fremont Island was the scene of two of the most interesting episodes of Great Salt Lake history. The first of these was the

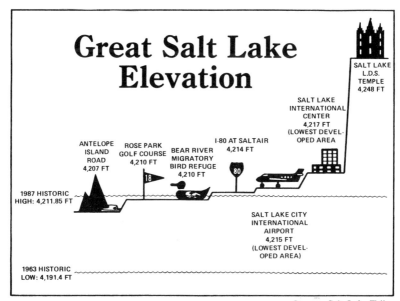

Great Salt Lake Elevation

SALT LAKE L.D.S. TEMPLE 4,248 FT

SALT LAKE INTERNATIONAL CENTER 4,217 FT (LOWEST DEVEL-OPED AREA)

ANTELOPE ISLAND ROAD 4,207 FT

ROSE PARK GOLF COURSE 4,210 FT

BEAR RIVER MIGRATORY BIRD REFUGE 4,210 FT

I-80 AT SALTAIR 4,214 FT

1987 HISTORIC HIGH: 4,211.85 FT

SALT LAKE CITY INTERNATIONAL AIRPORT 4,215 FT (LOWEST DEVEL-OPED AREA)

1963 HISTORIC LOW: 4,191.4 FT

Courtesy Salt Lake Tribune

exile of John Baptiste on that island in 1862. Baptiste had been hired as a grave digger at the Salt Lake City cemetery. However, because of some peculiar mental quirk in his make-up, he could not leave the dead buried and began digging into the graves and robbing the corpses. Some of the stolen articles of jewelry and clothing were then pawned in local shops and eventually put up for sale by the broker. Naturally, people soon began to recognize items they had buried with their loved ones. Thorough investigation and search revealed that Baptiste had robbed over 300 graves and had in his possession several boxes full of clothing taken from the dead.

The grave digger was tried and committed to exile on an island in the Great Salt Lake. Henry W. Miller, who then was using Fremont Island as a sheep range, assisted the sheriff in transporting the prisoner to that desolate place. Several weeks later, however, when the Millers returned to the island to make a routine check, Baptiste was gone. Apparently the exile had torn planks from the cabin for a raft and escaped to the mainland. He was never seen in the vicinity again.

Desert Island Home

From 1886 to 1891 Fremont Island was the scene of a much more dramatic episode—Judge U. J. Wenner of Salt Lake City decided to make the island a home for his family. Wenner and his young bride had moved from the east to Salt Lake City where he

Antelope Island Buffalo. During the 1920's the herd numbered more than 350.

became probate judge in 1882. However, he was afflicted with tuberculosis which grew gradually worse; his doctors advised complete rest and retirement from active life. Knowing Fremont Island, and hoping that the pure lake air would prove beneficial and possibly result in a cure, the judge sold his home in the city and moved with his wife and two small children to the desert island.

Island life seemed to agree with Judge Wenner and he decided to make a permanent home there. Rock was plentiful so with the aid of hired men, he built a two-story house, had his belongings shipped to the island, and stocked it with sheep and other livestock. Contact with the mainland was maintained by use of a boat which made regular trips for mail and supplies. In 1888 Mrs. Wenner, with her two small children, made a three-month trip to Illinois (the home of her parents) where a third child was born. Mother and children soon returned to the island home.

As the fifth year rolled around, Judge Wenner appeared to be getting along all right; at least he did not seem to be getting worse. Hence, a decision was made to spend a few months in California to give the islanders a taste of civilization. As final preparations for the vacation were being made, Judge Wenner had a sudden relapse and died. It was September 19, 1891, while the hired man was away to the mainland for mail and supplies that the final stroke came.

Mrs. Wenner, alone with three small children, bravely faced the crisis. She climbed the hill behind the house and lighted signal fires—the sign of distress—summoning the boatman to return at once. People on the mainland saw and recognized the fires two or three nights in succession but could do nothing to help. A heavy storm had come up and the boatman found it impossible to return to the island. Finally, however, the storm subsided and he was able to reach the island and learn the tragic news. Together he and Mrs. Wenner fashioned a coffin of rough lumber available on the spot and she lined it with a shawl. Between the two of them they managed to take the coffin to the brow of the hill behind the house and lower it into a grave. The children gathered white pebbles and marked the grave L O V E — a letter for each of the remaining members.

Within a few days the island home was deserted but not forgotten. Although Mrs. Wenner later re-married, she always held a very warm spot in her heart for the once happy island home. When she died (December 29, 1942) her daughter, Blanche H. Wenner, made arrangements to deposit the ashes of her mother beside her former husband's grave on Fremont Island. Today the grave site is surrounded by a combination wire and concrete fence; the graves are marked by a cairn built of rocks taken from the old stone house. A bronze plaque bears the vital statistics of those buried there.

D. E. Miller Photo

Ruins of the old Wenner home on Fremont Island.

Gravesite on Fremont Island. Insert: Plaque gives vital statistics concerning Judge U. J. Wenner and his wife who lie buried on the island they loved.

Two other islands have been homesteaded and occupied at times during the past century of lake history. In the 1890's Alfred Lambourne homesteaded Gunnison Island for the purpose of planting a vineyard. Although he spent the major part of a year there and planted 1,000 grape vines, nothing came of the venture; there was not enough rainfall to support the vines.

A more recent attempt at homesteading was on Carrington Island in 1932, where Charles Stoddard built a cabin and lived with his wife and three small children completely isolated from the rest of the world during winter weather. The purpose of this venture was to convert the island into a suitable sheep ranch. However, insufficient water, coupled with the constant menace of numerous coyotes, led to ultimate failure of the attempt and he sold his claims to stockmen then operating on Stansbury Island.

The islands have seen guano harvesters, prospectors, sportsmen, and bird lovers. But, except for Antelope and Fremont Island, they are as desolate and isolated today as they were a hundred years ago.

Bird Rookeries

Literally thousands of sea gulls and pelicans make their homes on the islands. There are also a few cormorants and herons. Hat Island, commonly called "Bird" Island has become well known to most Utahns because of gulls and pelicans normally nesting there. However, during the low lake levels of the 1930's and 1940's the birds deserted "Bird" Island in favor of Gunnison and Egg Islands. This was probably because the island became, in fact, a peninsula, a broad plain connecting it with the mainland to the west. Because of this, predatory animals had easy access to the rookeries.

Bird rookeries on Great Salt Lake Islands are inaccessible to most people and visits to the islands during the nesting season are discouraged. But an ideal place for bird observation is the Bear River Migratory Bird Refuge located immediately west of Brigham City. This refuge contains more than 64,000 acres, most of it diked to provide ideal habitats for various types of waterfowl. More than 40,000 ducks and 4,000 geese nest there each year. The refuge is a veritable sportsmen's paradise. It is estimated that 200 species of waterfowl, some of them very rare, visit the area annually. More swans are said to be found there than in any other place in the United States.

The Story of the Sea Gulls

Sea gulls have long been honored and protected by law in the state of Utah because of the part they played in destroying

Artesian Well, Fremont Island. Several fresh water wells have been drilled on Fremont Island from time to time. This one consists of one length of pipe—16 feet—pushed into the ground at lake level. Numerous fresh-water springs are located on Antelope Island.

D. E. Miller Photo

Courtesy W. H. Behle
Young cormorant in nest, Egg Island.

crickets that threatened to devastate crops in Salt Lake Valley during the spring and summer of 1848—the year after the coming of the Mormons to Utah. Food supplies were extremely low and the very lives of the settlers depended on bounteous harvests. Furthermore, thousands of new settlers were then on the way from various parts of the United States and Europe to join their fellow believers in the Salt Lake Valley. Failure of crops that year could have proved disastrous to the whole colonizing enterprise. Hence, it was with a great deal of anxiety that the new occupants of the valley sowed their grain and watched the tender shoots push through the surface of the ground. The grain came up beautifully and grew rapidly—everything pointed to a bounteous harvest. The pioneers, always a devout people, rejoiced and thanked God for his goodness.

Then one day there suddenly appeared an onslaught of hordes of large black crickets. These insects came from the foothills and moved relentlessly from field to field leaving each a desolate waste, devouring every green thing before them. All human attempts to halt and destroy the crickets failed—the black horde pushed deeper and deeper into the valley. Men, women, and children turned out to fight the pests. From daybreak until dark the struggle went on. Brooms, fences, shovels, ditches, fires—all were used, but to no avail. There seemed no end to the seething black mass of insects. Feeling that all human efforts could not stop the destructive horde, the faithful pioneers again turned to God, pleading for divine intervention to save the crops.

It was then that large flocks of sea gulls from their nesting grounds on Great Salt Lake islands began to make their appearance. As the gulls settled into the fields the fears of the settlers mounted; had the gulls come to complete the destruction? Fears were soon turned to thanksgiving, however, for the screaming birds fell upon the crickets and began to devour them. Gorging themselves with as many of the insects as they could possibly contain, flying to the lake and nearby streams, regurgitating the meal and returning again and again, the gulls soon put an end to the crickets. The crops were saved!

30

Courtesy Utah Fish & Game Commission
Young pelicans on Gunnison Island. Thousands of pelicans nest on
this Great Salt Lake island.

Courtesy Clyde Anderson
More than 60,000 seagulls nest on Great Salt Lake islands.

The Mormons, believing that a miracle had been performed in their behalf, had laws passed forbidding man to kill the gull in Utah, and erected a monument in its honor. This beautiful monument (said to be the first ever erected in honor of a bird) stands on Temple Square and bears the following inscription:

Sea Gull Monument Erected in Grateful Remembrance of the Mercy of God to the Mormon Pioneers

DISCOVERY AND EXPLORATION

The Escalante Expedition, 1776.

The first definite historical knowledge concerning the existence of Great Salt Lake came about as a result of the Dominguez-Escalante Expedition of 1776. This was a small band of Spanish missionary explorers headed by Francisco Atanacio Dominguez and Silvestre de Escalante. (Escalante kept an accurate record of the journey, hence it is usually called the Escalante Expedition.) The party left Santa Fe in search of a direct route to Monterey, California; a route that would avoid the Grand Canyon of the Colorado. Pioneering a course through western Colorado this group entered Utah and crossed the Green River near the present Dinosaur National Monument at Jensen, followed the Duchesne River westward to the present Strawberry Lake vicinity, struck the headwaters of a tributary of the Spanish Fork River and followed that stream to Utah Lake where they arrived September 23, 1776. Although Escalante did not explore northward from Utah Lake to Great Salt Lake he did learn from the Indians that such a large salty lake existed a short distance to the north. His maps depict it as a northern arm of Utah Lake. Escalante named the lake "Timpanogos," in honor of the natives found in the vicinity. That name stuck to the lake (and the river believed to feed and/or drain it) for half a century, although the name "Great Salt Lake" gradually gained popularity (during the 1820's and 1830's) among trappers who hunted beaver along the rivers feeding the lake. Early maps of the region, based entirely on hearsay, show large rivers flowing westward from Great Salt Lake into the Pacific Ocean.

James Bridger Discovers the Lake, 1824.

James Bridger, famous Rocky Mountain fur trapper, was the first white man known to have actually seen the waters of Great Salt Lake. That was late in 1824 when a group of William Henry

Mythical Rivers of the West. This is a small portion of an 1826 map showing two rivers (R. Los Mongos and R. Timpanogos) draining "Lake Timpanogos" as the Great Salt Lake was then called. Notice also "R. Buenaventura" running from eastern Utah through Sevier Lake (L. Salado) into San Francisco Bay. In 1843-44 John C. Fremont proved that there are no such rivers.

Ashley's men, while descending Bear River, placed wagers concerning the course of that stream and its point of discharge—whether into the ocean or some inland lake. When the fur brigade arrived in Cache Valley near Franklin, Idaho, young Bridger was sent to discover the answer.

Bridger reached the lake at the present location of the Bear River Migratory Bird Refuge. He dipped into the water, took a taste, spat it out with an oath, and returned to his companions to report that he had reached an arm of the Pacific. This fallacious belief was soon disproved, however, as the Rocky Mountain trappers plied their trade along the base of the Wasatch Range.

James Clyman Circumnavigates the Lake, 1826.

It was for the purpose of seeking new beaver streams and to determine the extent of the lake and whether or not it had an outlet to the west, that leaders of the Rocky Mountain Fur Company dispatched an exploring expedition of four men headed by James Clyman to circumnavigate the lake in bull boats during the summer of 1826. This exploring party left from the present site of Ogden and floated down Weber River to the lake. From that point they probably struck westward between Fremont Island and Promontory Point, skirted the north and west shores to the south end of the lake and eventually returned to rendezvous, having completely circumnavigated that body of water and having found no outlet or beaver-bearing streams.

This exploration took three weeks during which time the men suffered greatly from lack of drinking water. They found the whole west shore most desolate and completely devoid of fresh water. The past century has seen no material change in this situation—the west shore is as desolate as ever.

Captain Bonneville's Contribution to Great Salt Lake History

Ten years later further knowledge of the lake and the Great Basin was supplied by Captain B. L. E. Bonneville's reports and maps, published in 1837. Bonneville was an army officer who

Bonneville's Map, 1837. This is a portion of a map first published in 1837 as part of Captain Bonneville's journal, edited by Washington Irving and published under the title of *The Rocky Mountains*. This work was subsequently published under the title of *Adventures of Captain Bonneville*. This is the earliest map to show islands in the lake, although they are misplaced; it is the first to use the name of Bonneville in connection with the lake; it is the first to actually show major elements of what later became known as the Great Basin several years before Fremont gave it that title in 1844.

Courtesy Utah History Atlas

D. E. Miller Photo

Carson Cross, Fremont Island. Carved by Kit Carson, September 9, 1843. Inset: Shows actual size of the Cross. Dr. W. P. Miller is shown in the picture.

obtained leave (1831) to head a trapping and exploring expedition into the West. Although he spent three years in the West without ever seeing Great Salt Lake, he did, in 1833, send his chief scout and guide, Joseph R. Walker, with some forty men on a trapping expedition from Bear River to California via the north shores of the lake and the Humboldt River. This expedition proved definitely that the lake is truly an inland sea and that the Great Basin is indeed a *basin* with interior drainage only. Washington Irving obtained Bonneville's journal and based much of his book, *The Rocky Mountains* (1837), on that record. Attempts to attach Bonneville's name to Great Salt Lake failed although the ancient predecessor of Great Salt Lake was later named in his honor.

John C. Fremont Scientifically Examines the Lake, 1843 and 1845.

John C. Fremont contributed as much as any other explorer to the history and exploration of Great Salt Lake before the coming of the Mormons to its shores. With government support, Fremont was equipped to scientifically explore and examine the regions of the West. He twice visited the lake—in 1843 and 1845. Fremont obtained his first good view of the lake from "Little Mountain" west of Ogden. On that occasion he likened himself to Balboa as that famed explorer stood on the Isthmus of Panama and first beheld the Pacific Ocean. Fremont had heard a great deal about the lake and had determined to explore it. He had brought with him an 18-foot "India Rubber" boat in which the lake cruise was

35

to be made. This boat was made of rubberized canvas and contained several compartments—air sacks—that kept the craft afloat. A hand bellows supplied the air.

Fremont and four companions (including Kit Carson) floated into the lake via Weber River on September 9, 1843, and rowed to the nearest island (named Fremont Island by Howard Stansbury in 1850). The boat proved to be a frail craft indeed; as the waves began to roll, the seams (found to be pasted instead of sewed) began to part and one man had to be kept busy at the bellows to keep the boat afloat. Fremont ordered the men to row for their lives, an order they diligently obeyed under the circumstances. The party reached the island about noon.

From the island peak (800 feet above the water surface) Fremont made a survey of the lake using a spy glass and other instruments. He accidentally left the brass cover of his spy glass at the island peak and later made note of it in his journal. Almost everyone who has visited the island since then has searched for the lost cap. It was actually found during the 1860's by Jacob Miller, who was then using the island as a sheep range. But people who don't know this still continue the search.

While Fremont was completing his survey, Kit Carson and associates chiseled a small cross on the side of a peculiar rock formation near the summit. Fremont made no mention of the cross in his record and it was first noticed by Stansbury in 1850. Since that time the origin of the cross has been a matter of considerable speculation. Some attribute it to Peter Skene Ogden (who never visited the island), others claim that some Catholic priest must have carved it. However, a careful reading of Carson's account of his life (written about 1856) settles any question concerning the chiseler.

While in the lake region Fremont determined the elevation of the water surface, 4,200 feet above sea level; analyzed its waters, obtaining 14 pints of salt from five gallons of lake water; rode horseback to Antelope Island to hunt antelope (1845) and named that island; drew accurate maps of the vicinity; blazed what was to become known as Hastings Cutoff of later Donner fame; wrote accurate and interesting accounts of the lake and surrounding valleys, thus stimulating interest for further exploration and colonization there. The Mormons, when they were seeking a location for settlement in the West, studied Fremont's report very carefully and were, no doubt, influenced by it.

Three Lake Surveys

During the past century Great Salt Lake has been completely scientifically surveyed three different times. These surveys have consisted of complete lake soundings, accurate mapping of the shorelines and islands, study of the flora and fauna found in the lake vicinity, and an examination of the water, mineral and other natural resources. The first of these was the Stansbury Survey of 1849-50 under the direction of Howard Stansbury, who was sent to Utah by the U.S. Government for that purpose. During 1869-70 Clarence King, geologist of the Fortieth Parallel Survey, conducted the second complete examination of the lake—the King Survey. The third complete instrument survey was made in 1934-35 under the direction of Dr. Thomas C. Adams, then affiliated with the University of Utah, and is commonly known as the Adams Survey.

These surveys give us an excellent picture of the lake as it has been most of the time during the past century. The King Survey of 1870 found the lake at nearly its highest recorded level; it had almost reached its all-time low in 1935 when the Adams Survey was made; when Stansbury examined the lake in 1850 it stood about midway between these two extremes.

Numerous partial surveys and lake soundings have been made from time to time. There will be many more in the future.

BARRIER TO WESTWARD MIGRATION

During the westward migration a century ago Great Salt Lake was a forbidding barrier; immigrants to California had to by-pass it either to the north or the south. The Bartleston-Bidwell party of 1841 blazed a trail around its north and west shores to Pilot Peak, being the first white men to reach that point. But their sufferings were so severe and the region so desolate that no one tried to follow their trail. Southwest of Pilot Peak in Nevada they finally abandoned their wagons and "packed in" to California.

The Donner Party

In 1846 the Donner party, so well known in the annals of the West, made their famous trek over Hastings Cutoff. This company, consisting of some 80 people was seduced from the main California trail at Ft. Bridger in favor of a supposed easy short-cut via the south shores of the lake that would reportedly cut some 300 miles off the long California road.

From springs located 15 miles south of Timpie the trail turned northwestward. After a superhuman struggle all the immigrants managed to reach the springs at Pilot Peak, 80 miles away. But many horses and oxen and several wagons had to be abandoned in the sticky mud of the salty wastes.

It was the great delay and hardships in the Wasatch Mountains and on the Salt Desert that spelled ultimate tragedy for the Donner party. They finally reached the Sierras (west of Reno) too late to cross because of early snows. Thirty-four of their number fell victims of starvation, freezing, and cannibalism. After the Donner experience, most California-bound immigrants who came via Salt Lake City, chose a longer safer route around the north end of the lake, striking the regular California trail at Junction Valley in Southern Idaho.

It was not until 1907 that the Western Pacific Railroad constructed a line across the salt flats to Wendover. In 1925 U.S. Highway 40 between Salt Lake City and Wendover was completed.

Lucin Cutoff

The first transcontinental railroad had to by-pass Great Salt Lake. Union Pacific, building from the east, and Central Pacific from the west, followed a course around the north end of the lake, meeting at Promontory (not Promontory Point) May 10, 1869. But the line was full of curves and steep grades. Long before 1900 this had developed into the chief bottleneck of the whole transcontinental line, and Southern Pacific Railroad officials planned the famous Lucin Cutoff from Ogden directly west across the lake to Lucin near the west Utah border. After having made complete lake soundings and surveys, construction of the new route was begun in March, 1902. Approach to either side of the lake was relatively simple; the real task began when the first piles were driven in Great Salt Lake August 2, 1902.

The original Cutoff consists chiefly of a rock and gravel fill through shallow lake brine. However, approximately 12 miles of trestle and a 600-foot bridge at Bear River Bay span the deeper waters. Much of the fill had to be built from temporary trestles constructed on piles driven into the lake bed. However, it was the construction of the fills, rather than the trestle, that caused most of the construction headaches. Train load after train load of solid rock and gravel simply disappeared into the soft mud below the water. Eventually, however, enough solid materials were poured into the lake to provide a substantial bed for the rails. Materials for these fills were obtained from both sides of the lake and from Promontory Point. Extreme hardship was encountered on the west side where all supplies—even fresh water amounting to 420,000 gallons a day—had to be hauled an average of about 100 miles.

Almost 23 miles of trestle were constructed although only about half of it was intended to be permanent. In all, 28,250 piles were driven; trees used varied in height from 100 to 150 feet.

Many acres of forest went into the Cutoff. Water in the permanent trestle section varied from 30 to 34 feet in depth and piles had to be driven many feet into the lake bottom in order to insure a stable structure. When "soft spots" were struck a 100-foot pile could often be driven out of sight without striking solid footing.

Courtesy Southern Pacific Railroad
Lucin Cutoff. Pile drivers working from both sides of the lake met at "Mid-lake" in 1903.

Courtesy KUED
Poles as long as 120 feet were used as piling for the Lucin Cutoff.

In such places it was necessary to lash two piles together and drive them into the lake in order to make a solid trestle.

Piles were driven 15 feet apart in rows of five. The tops of each set of piles were joined crosswise by a beam 12 inches square and 18 feet long. Each set of piles was then connected to the next set by a dozen similar timbers running lengthwise of the right-of-way. On top of this sturdy framework a floor of three-inch lumber created a base on which a coat of asphalt was placed. On top of this a foot of rock ballast formed a solid base in which the ties were placed. This gravel ballast made it much easier to lay a perfectly level track. The roadbed thus created was 16 feet wide and approximately 18 feet above the water. The piling has become thoroughly "pickled" by the lake brine and is just as solid today as when the construction was completed in 1903.

The Lucin Cutoff shortened the rail distance from Ogden to Lucin by 43.77 miles and the time by 7 hours. It cut out 3,919 degrees of curvature (enough to turn a train around almost 11 times), and eliminated 1,515 feet of grade. The sharpest curve on the new line is a curve of only 1.5 degrees (at Promontory Point) compared with curves of 10 degrees on the old line. The Lucin Cutoff actually runs 36 miles without any grade and 30 additional miles (west of the lake) with a very slight grade—21 feet to the mile. Compare this with the 90 feet to the mile grade on the old line and the advantages become more obvious. It is so straight, so level, and so long that the curvature of the earth can actually be observed on it.

During the 1950's the trestle portion of the cutoff was replaced with a solid rock and gravel fill at a cost of more than $50,000,000. During construction several tugs and barges (the Great Salt Lake Fleet) transported the materials from Little Valley

Great Salt Lake Fleet. During the construction of the new Lucin Cutoff barges and tugboats were used to transport fill material from the Promontory Range to the fill site in the lake.

Courtesy KUED

on the West side of the Promontory range and dropped it along a line a short distance north of the old trestle.

Building the Lucin Cutoff must be considered one of the greatest feats of railroad construction.

Courtesy Southern Pacific Railroad
Original Lucin Cutoff, Great Salt Lake. "Going to Sea by Rail."

LAKE BONNEVILLE, PREDECESSOR OF GREAT SALT LAKE

Length . . . . 346 miles
Width . . . . 145 miles
Area . . . . 19,750 sq. miles
Depth . . . . 1,050 feet

The Great Salt Lake is "great" in the sense that it is the largest salt lake in America and the largest lake in the United States west of the Mississippi River. However, it is only a small remnant of its ancient predecessor, Lake Bonneville, which covered an area ten times as great as the present lake some 20,000 to 100,000 years ago. This ancient lake was formed during periods of excessive precipitation in the Great Basin primarily during the fourth glacial period of geological time. Geologists point out that there were tremendous climatic changes during that geological epoch, that there were times of abundant rainfall followed by long periods of drought. But the overall trend showed an increased precipitation that pushed the lake level upward. The time element was tremendous. The lake is believed to have climbed almost to the rim of the basin and then dried up completely two or three times before it finally attained its greatest height and flowed over the basin rim at Red Rock Pass in present day southern Idaho.

At its highest stage Lake Bonneville waters spread over 12,640,000 acres which included many of the most fertile valleys of Utah, and buried the present locations of towns and cities where a million people now live. It covered parts of a dozen counties in Utah, Idaho, and Nevada (some of them almost completely). If the lake were to rise again to its former level (which is impossible because the outlet is more than three hundred feet below the high water mark) Utah's four largest cities would be submerged: Salt Lake City, 850 feet; Ogden, 850 feet; Provo, 650 feet; Logan, 500 feet. Towns and cities near the present shores of Great Salt Lake such as Kelton, Saltair, Hooper, Syracuse, and Promontory Point, would lie under 1,000 feet of water, for Lake Bonneville was 1,000 feet deeper than Great Salt Lake is today. Bingham would be a lake shipping port.

At its highest water level, Lake Bonneville covered 19,750 square miles, was 346 miles long, 145 miles wide, and reached a depth of 1,050 feet. This area is comparable to the combined areas of Rhode Island, Connecticut, Massachusetts, and half of New Hampshire. In its heyday Lake Bonneville compared favorably with present day lakes of the United States as the accompanying table shows.

COMPARATIVE DIMENSIONS OF LAKES IN THE UNITED STATES

	Area	Length	Width	Extreme Depth
Lake Bonneville	19,750 sq. mi.	346 mi.	145 mi.	1,050 ft.
Great Salt Lake	1,500 sq. mi.	75 mi.	50 mi.	34 ft.
Lake Superior	31,800 sq. mi.	350 mi.	170 mi.	1,180 ft.
Lake Huron	23,010 sq. mi.	206 mi.	215 mi.	750 ft.
Lake Michigan	22,400 sq. mi.	307 mi.	106 mi.	870 ft.
Lake Erie	9,940 sq. mi.	241 mi.	58 mi.	210 ft.
Lake Ontario	7,540 sq. mi.	193 mi.	67 mi.	738 ft.

The shoreline of Lake Bonneville, a thousand feet above the level of Great Salt Lake, formed an intricate pattern of bays, estuaries and peninsulas. Most of the present islands of the lake were submerged and many of the present mountains were surrounded by water; Pilot Peak, for example, was an island as was most of the Promontory range. The main body of the ancient lake was in the present Salt Lake Valley, Tooele and Rush Valleys, and the Great Salt Lake Desert. To the south extended Utah Bay where Utah Lake remains, a fresh water remnant of ancient Bonneville. Other bays reached farther west and south, the most important of which was the Sevier Body where Sevier Lake is found today. Escalante Bay extended still farther southward to within about 50 miles of the Utah-Arizona state line. To the

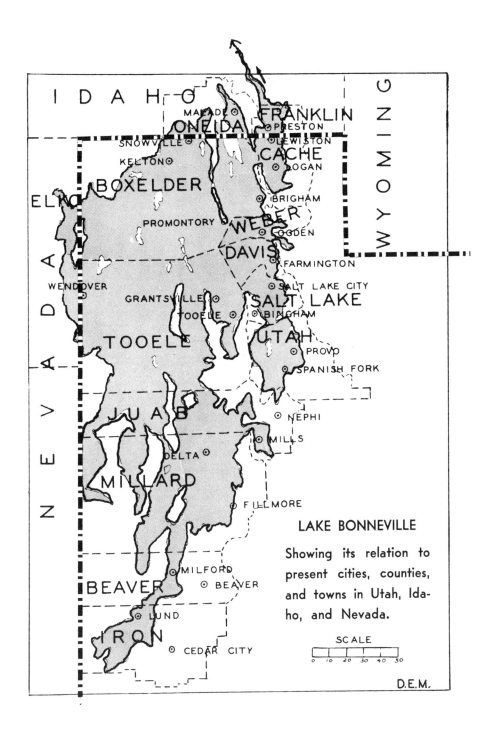

IDAHO

WYOMING

NEVADA

ELKO

ONEIDA

MALADE
PRESTON
FRANKLIN

SNOWVILLE
LEWISTON
CACHE
KELTON
LOGAN

BOXELDER
BRIGHAM

PROMONTORY
WEBER
OGDEN

DAVIS
FARMINGTON

WENDOVER
SALT LAKE CITY

GRANTSVILLE
SALT LAKE
TOOELE
BINGHAM
UTAH

TOOELE
PROVO
SPANISH FORK

JUAB
NEPHI

MILLS

DELTA

MILLARD
FILLMORE

MILFORD
BEAVER

BEAVER
LUND

IRON
CEDAR CITY

LAKE BONNEVILLE

Showing its relation to
present cities, counties,
and towns in Utah, Ida-
ho, and Nevada.

SCALE
0 10 20 30 40 50

D.E.M.

43

northeast, Cache Bay projected itself into present day Cache Valley. It was through this bay that the lake found its outlet at Red Rock Pass.

To Grove Karl Gilbert, geologist of the Wheeler Survey (1869-70) goes the credit for having thoroughly surveyed and explored the ancient shorelines. Gilbert and his men carefully followed the various terraces and mapped them accurately until he was able to assert that the ancient lake was probably as well known as many modern lakes lying in remote regions. It was Gilbert who located the outlet at Red Rock Pass. He it was, also, who named the lake in honor of Captain B. L. E. Bonneville, whom he assumed had explored the Great Salt Lake region in 1833. In reality, Captain Bonneville spent three years in the West without coming nearer than 50 miles to the Great Salt Lake. Gilbert's monograph, *Lake Bonneville* (published in 1890), is still the masterpiece and chief source of information concerning that ancient lake.

The shorelines of Lake Bonneville are so striking that even the most casual visitor cannot help but notice them; no geological training is necessary for such observation. Rather than obscure marks on the hills, these lines form distinct terraces on the mountain sides surrounding the present lake. Howard Stansbury was the first to make note of the terraces when he observed them on the Terrace Mountains near the northwest corner of the lake in 1849. As he continued his survey the following year, he was further impressed by the various terraces found in numerous places on the mountains and islands of the lake vicinity. A study of the terraces convinced Stansbury and others that the lake had remained at various levels relatively long periods of time as indicated by the prominent shorelines, often worn into solid rock by wave action of the prehistoric lake.

Although some 50 terraces are visible at various points on the mountains surrounding Salt Lake Valley, the three most outstanding ones are the Bonneville, Provo, and Stansbury terraces. The most prominent of all, chiefly because of its height, is the Bonneville terrace visible on the mountain above Magna and very prominent on the Wasatch range north, east and south of Salt Lake City. Just above Ft. Douglas and St. Mary's-of-the-Wasatch the line is clearly visible and can be followed without difficulty south to the Traverse Mountains east of the Jordan Narrows. Near the site of the Utah State prison it is exceptionally prominent. This terrace stands approximately 1,000 feet above the present level of Great Salt Lake and indicates that the water must have stood at that level for a great length of time before rising high enough to run over the basin rim at Red Rock Pass. Once an outlet

Bonneville Terrace. This picture shows the terrace formed by ancient Lake Bonneville. This view is seen in the south end of Salt Lake Valley.

Excursion to Midlake on the Lucin Cutoff trestle about 1908. "Going to Sea by Rail" was quite popular after the completion of the Lucin Cutoff. Partially because of the fire danger, the Midlake station was removed long before the old trestle was replaced by the solid rock and gravel fill of the new Lucin Cutoff.

was reached the water cut rapidly down some 375 feet, draining the lake to the Provo level.

Grove Karl Gilbert estimated that the outflowing stream was about the size of Niagara River and drained the lake to the Provo level in about 25 years, cutting down rapidly through alluvial soil to a bed of limestone which arrested further deepening of the channel. The outflowing Bonneville River followed the route of present day Portneuf, Snake, and Columbia Rivers to the Pacific Ocean.

The Provo level stands 625 feet above the present surface of Great Salt Lake and was so named because of the Provo delta which it formed. This delta is locally known as Provo Bench; U.S. Highway 91 passes over it for several miles in the Orem vicinity. The Provo terrace far surpasses in strength the Bonneville terrace above it, indicating that the lake remained at the Provo level an exceedingly long time. It is very prominent on the Oquirrh Mountains above Magna, on Antelope Island and the Promontory range. On the east bench in Salt Lake City the Provo level is not so well defined, but it would follow a line approximately where Wasatch Drive crosses Ft. Douglas. At the Provo level the lake's area was 13,000 square miles. Its water was not saline since it maintained a constant overflow through Red Rock Pass.

The third important level of Lake Bonneville was reached when, because of changing climatic conditions and decreasing precipitation, its waters dropped more than 300 feet to reach the Stansbury level. At that time the lake was 330 feet deeper than present Great Salt Lake and covered 7,000 square miles (more than four times the area of the present lake). Since this level was reached as a result of evaporation, all the salt and other minerals tended to become more concentrated and the lake began to assume its salty characteristics. By that time the lake had withdrawn from all the southern bays and was concentrated in the basin now occupied by Great Salt Lake and the Great Salt Lake Desert to the west.

Since the time of the Provo level the lake has declined to its present size because evaporation exceeded precipitation during most of the time. Numerous minor terraces mark levels at which the lake maintained itself long enough for its waters to make impressions on the islands and mountains of the lake basin.

Lake Bonneville was a fresh water lake during its higher stages and it seems likely that numerous species of fish and other marine life should have lived in it. Yet, with the exception of large numbers of gastropods (soft-shelled animals), no fossil remains of marine animal life have been found in the old lake bed. Future discoveries may possibly change this picture completely.

However, various types of prehistoric animals are known to have roamed the *shores* of that ancient lake. As might be expected, many of these were trapped in the sands along the shores and sank into the depths to become fossils for study in our day. Remains of mammoths, musk oxen, camels, horses, deer and mountain sheep have been found at numerous places in deposits of the Bonneville basin, indicating an abundance of such animal life during the Bonneville era—twenty to fifty thousand years ago. No evidence of human habitation in the Bonneville vicinity (that would date back to the high water epoch) has been found.

WHAT IS TO BECOME OF THE LAKE?

What does the future hold in store for the lake? During the early 1960's when the historical low was reached, most concern about the lake was that it might dry up almost completely leaving large areas of exposed wasteland.

However, during the 1970's, as the lake rose higher than it had been for 50 years, both government and private agencies became alarmed about the impact of possible flooding on evaporation ponds and other installations used in extracting minerals from the brine. During the five year period from March 30, 1982 to March 30, 1987, record precipitation caused the lake to rise an unprecedented 12 feet. The official recorded high as measured by the USGS on March 30, 1987, was 4,211.85 feet above sea level. This level surpassed the previous 1873 historic high of 4,211.6 feet and exceeded the 1963 low of 4,191.35 feet by 20½ feet.

Due to the flat areas surrounding the shoreline of the Great Salt Lake, this 12 foot rise in the water level increased the surface area about 900 square miles. The resulting extensive flooding caused more than 200 million dollars in damages, including the flooding and erosion of both Interstate 80 and the Southern Pacific Railroad Causeway. The road between Syracuse and the Utah State Park on Antelope Island was completely inundated. In addition, evaporation ponds and other mineral extraction facilities were ruined. Flooding of sewage treatment plants threatened public health, wildlife habitat was destroyed, and extensive damage was done to private property.

As the lake continued to rise, state officials had no choice but to take action. The risk of further damage was too great to allow the luxury of waiting for a dry weather cycle. A multimillion dollar pumping project to transfer lake water into the western Great Salt Lake desert was selected as the most feasible means of keeping the lake level in check. Some solutions which were considered and rejected were more extensive diking, additional dams to control the rivers that feed the lake, and diversion of the Bear River into the Columbia River drainage system.

The West Desert Pumping Project is situated on the western shore of the lake and cost $60 million to construct. It was completed in only 9 ½ months. A canal 60 feet deep and 25 feet wide was carved through four miles of dirt and rock into a shallow evaporation basin [average depth 3 feet], about one fifth the size of the Great Salt Lake itself.

Three huge pumps with impellers ten feet in diameter lifted water 15 feet up out of the lake at the rate of 1.6 million gallons per minute. Each pump was powered by a 16-cylinder natural gas engine. Reduction in the size of the lake was to be achieved by enlarging the surface area, which would increase evaporation. Since the Great Salt Lake has no outlet, evaporation is the sole means by which the lake loses water.

The pumps operated from April 1987 until June 30 1989. During this time the level of the lake dropped more than six feet due to the combination of pumping and arid weather. After the pumps were stopped, care was taken to preserve them indefinitely for possible future use. The cylinders were coated with protective oil and lines were filled with nitrogen gas to prevent rusting. The impellers remain underwater since they were manufactured with special alloys impervious to salt water.

The dry cycle starting in mid 1987 led to a unprecedented decline in the depth of the lake which could lead to historical lows. When will this trend end? Will the pumps be needed again?

D. E. Miller Photo

Lakemobile. During the 1940's, when the lake was low, Charles Stoddard converted this truck into a "Lakemobile" in which he navigated the lake between Syracuse and Fremont Island. The machine was used for several years.